Summary

North Korea has been among the most vexing and persistent problems in U.S. foreign policy in the post-Cold War period. The United States has never had formal diplomatic relations with the Democratic People's Republic of Korea (the official name for North Korea). Negotiations over North Korea's nuclear weapons program have consumed the past three U.S. administrations, even as some analysts anticipated a collapse of the isolated authoritarian regime. North Korea has been the recipient of well over $1 billion in U.S. aid and the target of dozens of U.S. sanctions.

This report provides background information on the negotiations over North Korea's nuclear weapons program that began in the early 1990s under the Clinton Administration. As U.S. policy toward Pyongyang evolved through the George W. Bush presidency and into the Obama Administration, the negotiations moved from mostly bilateral to the multilateral Six-Party Talks (made up of China, Japan, Russia, North Korea, South Korea, and the United States). Although the negotiations have reached some key agreements that lay out deals for aid and recognition to North Korea in exchange for denuclearization, major problems with implementation have persisted. With talks suspended since 2009, concern about proliferation to other actors has grown.

After Kim Jong-il's sudden death in December 2011, the reclusive regime now faces the challenge of transferring dynastic power to his youngest son, Kim Jong-un. Pyongyang had shown signs of reaching out in 2011 after a string of provocative acts in 2010, including an alleged torpedo attack on a South Korean warship that killed 46 South Korean servicemen and an artillery attack on Yeonpyeong Island that killed two South Korean Marines and two civilians. When Kim passed, the United States was reportedly on the verge of announcing an agreement on food aid and Pyongyang had indicated a willingness to freeze some parts of its nuclear program.

The Obama Administration, like its predecessors, faces fundamental decisions on how to approach North Korea. To what degree should the United States attempt to isolate the regime diplomatically and financially? Should those efforts be balanced with engagement initiatives that continue to push for steps toward denuclearization, or for better human rights behavior? Should the United States adjust its approach in the post-Kim Jong-il era? Is China a reliable partner in efforts to pressure Pyongyang? Have the North's nuclear tests and alleged torpedo attack demonstrated that regime change is the only way to peaceful resolution? How should the United States consider its alliance relationships with Japan and South Korea as it formulates its North Korea policy? Should the United States continue to offer humanitarian aid?

Although the primary focus of U.S. policy toward North Korea is the nuclear weapons program, there are a host of other issues, including Pyongyang's missile program, illicit activities, and poor human rights record. Modest attempts at engaging North Korea, including joint operations to recover U.S. servicemen's remains from the Korean War and some discussion about opening a U.S. liaison office in Pyongyang, remain suspended along with the nuclear negotiations.

This report will be updated periodically. (This report covers the overall U.S.-North Korea relationship, with an emphasis on the diplomacy of the Six-Party Talks. For information on the technical issues involved in North Korea's weapons programs and delivery systems, as well as the steps involved in denuclearization, please see the companion piece to this report, CRS Report RL34256, *North Korea's Nuclear Weapons: Technical Issues*, by Mary Beth Nikitin. Please refer to the list at the end of this report for the full list of CRS reports focusing on other North Korean issues.)

Contents

Latest Developments: Kim Jong-il's Death 1
    Succession Process 1
    International Reaction 1
    Prospects for Reform, Provocations, and/or Return to Negotiations 1
Introduction 4
    Overview of Past U.S. Policy on North Korea 4
Obama Administration North Korea Policy 5
    Food Aid Debate Within U.S. Government 7
    North Korean Behavior During Obama Administration 7
        Pattern of Conciliation and Provocations 7
        String of Provocations in 2010 8
        Reaching Out Again in 2011 9
Six-Party Talks 9
    Background: History of Negotiations 9
    China's Role 10
North Korea's Internal Situation 11
    Succession Process 12
    Solidifying Ties with China 13
Other U.S. Concerns with North Korea 13
    North Korea's Human Rights Record 13
        North Korean Refugees 14
        The North Korean Human Rights Act 15
        Implementation 15
    North Korea's Illicit Activities 16
    North Korea's Missile Program 17
U.S. Engagement Activities with North Korea 18
    U.S. Assistance to North Korea 18
    POW-MIA Recovery Operations in North Korea 18
    Potential for Establishing a Liaison Office in North Korea 19
    Non-Governmental Organizations' Activities 19
List of Other CRS Reports on North Korea 20
        Archived Reports for Background 21

Figures

Figure 1. Korean Peninsula 3

Contacts

Author Contact Information 21
Acknowledgments 21

Latest Developments: Kim Jong-il's Death

Kim Jong-il, North Korea's leader since 1994, died suddenly on December 17, reportedly from a heart attack onboard a train. His death forced Pyongyang to accelerate the succession process that had been underway since Kim's reported stroke in 2008. The military and party elite have confirmed the designation of Kim's youngest son, Kim Jong-un, as successor to his father and worked assiduously to install the younger Kim as the undisputed leader. Kim appears to be surrounded by a group of established senior figures, leading to speculation that North Korea may adopt a collective leadership system as the ruler establishes himself.

Succession Process

As the weeks since Kim's death have passed, Kim Jong-un, believed to be 27 or 28 years of age, has received several new titles: among them, the "Supreme Commander" of the Korean People's Army (KPA). Unlike his father, he has not been named as Chairman of the National Defense Commission, nor to the top post of the Workers' Party of Korea (WPK), but he has been described by official state organs as the "sole national leader," leaving little doubt that he has consolidated power at the outset. A month after Kim's passing, most observers note that the transfer of authority appears to have executed smoothly, with little indication of power struggles between the party and the military, two traditional centers of power in Pyongyang. Despite the apparent consensus on the new leader, many analysts caution that competition among different groups of elites may break out in the months to come.

International Reaction

Other capitals' reactions have emphasized stability in the wake of Kim's death. Beijing almost immediately bestowed legitimacy on the new leadership by sending regards at the highest level, as well as dispatching a stream of high-level officials to pay respects at Pyongyang's embassy in Beijing. Seoul and Washington have also been careful to avoid raising alarm that may trigger a violent response from North Korea. Both capitals issued carefully worded statements expressing concern for the people of North Korea. Despite this restraint, pronouncements from Pyongyang have made clear that the new leadership does not envision a rapid detente with South Korea; shortly after Kim's death, the state-run news agency carried a statement that labeled Seoul's rulers as "puppets" and bluntly warned other countries that there would be no change in North Korea's policy toward the South. North Korea has also accused the United States of politicizing the humanitarian aid issue, but has refrained from using its most aggressive language.

Prospects for Reform, Provocations, and/or Return to Negotiations

Analysts differ on whether the transfer of power offers opportunity for renewed engagement with the reclusive state. Optimists point to the fact that Kim is young and was partially educated at European schools, which may make him more open to economic and political reform and international outreach. Multiple sources claim that Beijing considers Jang Song-taek, vice-chairman of the National Defense Commission and Kim's uncle, to be friendly to economic reform. Others point out that Kim's novice status likely makes him more beholden to established interests in the elite and that the regime may in fact be more likely to launch attacks or other provocations as a result. If Kim is eager to prove his hard-line credentials with the powerful military, for example, he may be willing to carry out another nuclear test or another act of aggression.

On the other hand, North Korea has an acute need for aid, particularly ahead of the expected celebration of founder Kim Il-sung's 100th birthday in April 2012. For this reason, many analysts anticipate that after a period of grieving, the regime will resume bilateral negotiations with the United States, and return to the tentative North-South dialogue with Seoul. According to press reports, the United States was on the verge of announcing a substantial food aid donation to North Korea at the time of Kim Jong-il's death and Pyongyang may agree to halting the uranium enrichment portion of its nuclear program. Such an agreement would likely have been a precursor to a return to the multilateral disarmament negotiations known as the Six-Party Talks. The question of resuming these talks under Kim Jong-un also remains unclear, but likely depends on the same factors, namely the need to court more international aid. Many analysts are convinced that North Korea has little intention of giving up its nuclear weapons, but may be more willing to negotiate parts of its program and curb more provocations through the negotiations.

Figure 1. Korean Peninsula

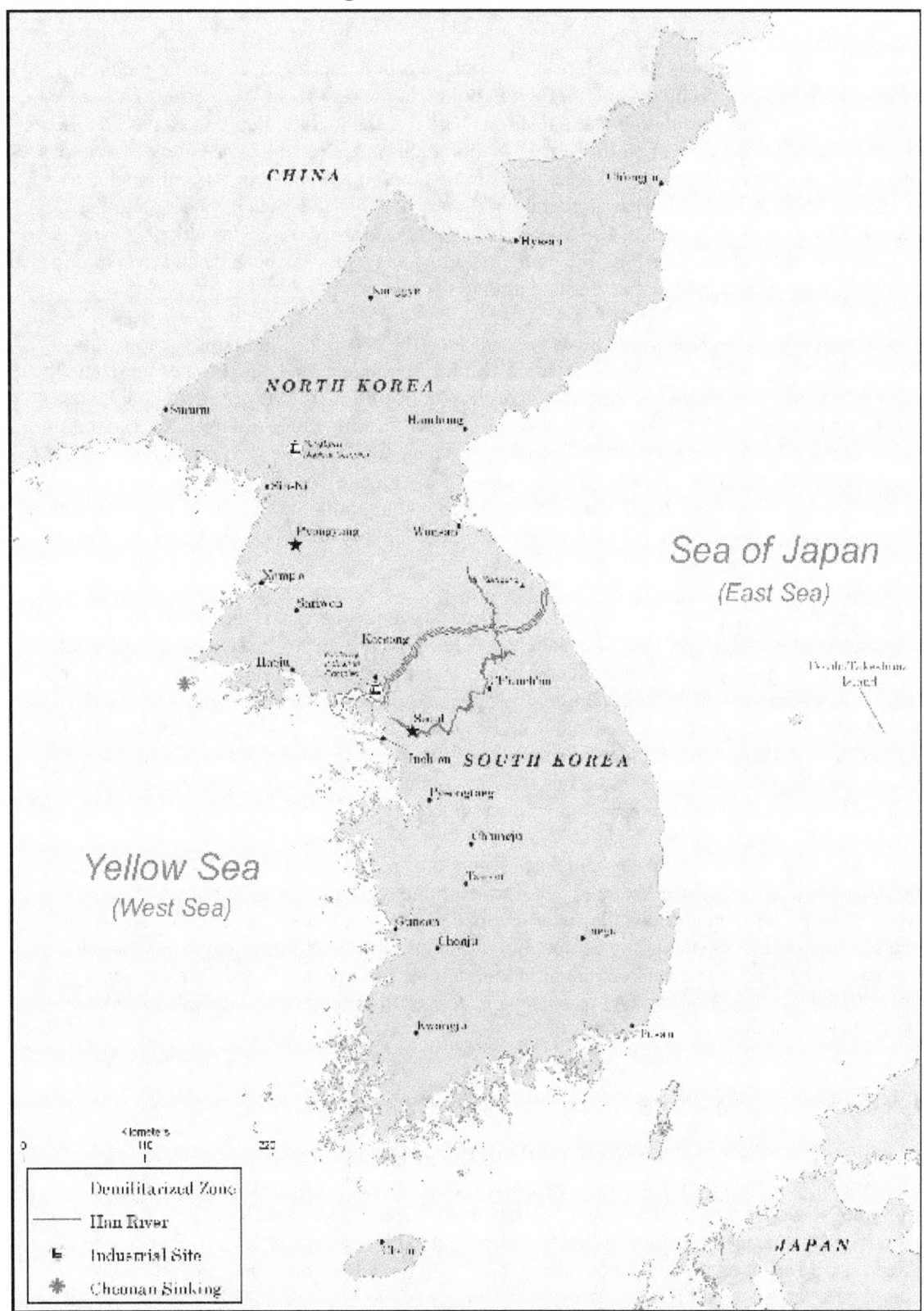

Source: Prepared by CRS based on ESRI Data and Maps 9.3.1; IHS World Data.

Introduction

An impoverished nation of about 23 million people, North Korea has been among the most vexing and persistent problems in U.S. foreign policy in the post-Cold War period. The United States has never had formal diplomatic relations with the Democratic People's Republic of Korea (DPRK, the official name for North Korea). Negotiations over North Korea's nuclear weapons program have consumed the past three administrations, even as some analysts anticipated a collapse of the isolated authoritarian regime in Pyongyang. North Korea has been both the recipient of billions of dollars of U.S. aid and the target of dozens of U.S. sanctions. Once considered a relic of the Cold War, the divided Korean peninsula has become an arena of more subtle strategic and economic competition among the region's powers.

U.S. interests in North Korea encompass crucial security, economic, and political concerns. Bilateral military alliances with South Korea and Japan obligate the United States to defend these allies from any attack from the North. Tens of thousands of U.S. troops occupying the largest U.S. military bases in the Pacific are stationed within proven striking range of North Korean missiles. An outbreak of conflict on the Korean peninsula or the collapse of the government in Pyongyang would have severe implications for the regional—if not global—economy. Negotiations and diplomacy surrounding North Korea's nuclear weapons program influence U.S. relations with all the major powers in the region and have become a particularly complicating factor for Sino-U.S. ties.

At the center of this complicated intersection of geostrategic interests is the task of dealing with an isolated authoritarian regime, now under the additional pressure of executing a transfer of power following the death of leader Kim Jong-il. Unfettered by many of the norms that govern international diplomacy, the leadership in Pyongyang, now headed by its dynastic "Great Successor" Kim Jong-un, is unpredictable and opaque. So little is known about the new leader that the uncertainty surrounding policymaking in Pyongyang may be more murky than it was under Kim Jong-il. U.S. policymakers face a daunting challenge in navigating a course toward a peaceful resolution of the nuclear issue with a rogue actor.

In the long run, the ideal outcome remains, presumably, reunification of the Korean peninsula under stable democratic rule. At this point, however, the road to that result appears fraught with risks. If the Pyongyang regime falls due to internal or external forces, the potential for major strategic consequences (including competition for control of the North's nuclear arsenal) and a massive humanitarian crisis, not to mention long-term economic and social repercussions, loom large. In the interim, policymakers face deep challenges in even defining achievable objectives, let alone reaching them.

Overview of Past U.S. Policy on North Korea

Over the past decade, U.S. policy toward North Korea has ranged from direct bilateral engagement to labeling Pyongyang as part of an "axis of evil." Despite repeated provocations from the North, since 1994 there is no publicly available evidence that any U.S. administration has seriously considered a direct military strike or an explicit policy of regime change due to the threat of a devastating war on the peninsula. Although there have been periodic efforts to negotiate a "grand bargain" that addresses the full range of concerns with Pyongyang's behavior and activities, North Korea's nuclear program has usually been prioritized above North Korea's human rights record, its missile program, and its illicit and criminal dealings.

Even as the strategic and economic landscape of East Asia has undergone dramatic changes, North Korea has endured as a major U.S. foreign policy challenge. As Washington has shifted from a primarily bilateral (during the Clinton Administration) to a mostly multilateral framework (during the Bush and Obama Administrations) for addressing North Korea, the centrality of China's role in dealing with Pyongyang has become increasingly pronounced. North Korea is dependent on China's economic aid and diplomatic support for its survival. (See "China's Role" section below.) Cooperation on North Korea has competed with other U.S. policy priorities with Beijing such as Iran, currency adjustment, climate change, and human rights.

Relations with other countries, particularly Japan and South Korea, also influence U.S. policy toward North Korea; power transitions in other capitals can bring about shifts in the overall cooperation to deal with Pyongyang. In recent years, Japan's approach to North Korea has been harder-line than that of other Six-Party participants. South Korean President Lee Myung-bak is seen as more hawkish on Pyongyang than his recent predecessors, particularly since the sinking of the *Cheonan* in March 2010.

Identifying patterns in North Korean behavior is challenging, as Pyongyang often weaves together different approaches to the outside world. North Korean behavior has vacillated between limited cooperation and overt provocations, including testing two nuclear devices and several missiles between 2006 and 2009. Pyongyang's willingness to negotiate has often appeared to be driven by its internal conditions: food shortages or economic desperation can push North Korea to re-engage in talks, usually to extract more aid from China or, in the past, from South Korea. North Korea has proven skillful at exploiting divisions among the other five parties or taking advantage of political transitions in Washington to stall the Six-Party Talks negotiating process.

At the core of the North Korean issue is the question of what Pyongyang's leadership ultimately seeks. As the negotiations have endured dozens of twists and turns, analysts have remained divided on whether the regime truly seeks acceptance into (or is capable of entering) the international community, or remains resolutely committed to its existence as a closed society with nuclear weapons as a guarantor. If the latter, debate rages on the proper strategic response, with options ranging from trying to squeeze the dictatorship to the point of collapse to buying time and trying to prevent proliferation or other severely destabilizing events.

Obama Administration North Korea Policy

Beginning with his presidential campaign, Obama indicated a willingness to engage with "rogue" governments. Although not mentioning North Korea by name, he pledged in his inaugural address to reach out to isolated regimes. With a commitment to retaining the six-nation forum, U.S. officials have stated that they seek a comprehensive package deal for North Korea's complete denuclearization, which would include normalization of relations and significant aid.

However, a series of provocations from Pyongyang after Obama took office halted progress on furthering negotiations. In 2009, the North tested a second nuclear device, expelled U.S. and international nuclear inspectors, and declared it would "never" return to the talks. In response to the test, the United Nations Security Council unanimously passed Resolution 1874, which outlines a series of sanctions to deny financial benefits to the regime in Pyongyang.[1] As these

---

[1] For more information, see CRS Report R40684, *North Korea's Second Nuclear Test: Implications of U.N. Security* (continued...)

events played out, the Obama Administration adopted what Secretary of State Hillary Clinton dubbed a "strategic patience" policy that essentially waits for North Korea to come back to the table while maintaining pressure through economic sanctions and arms interdictions. Critics claim that this approach has allowed Pyongyang to control the situation, while fears of further nuclear advances and possible proliferation build. While the talks are frozen, Washington has maintained a strong united approach with Seoul and Tokyo. Despite reports of China's harsh reaction to North Korea's provocations, and Beijing support for adoption of U.N. Security Council Resolution 1874, Beijing has remained unwilling to impose more stringent economic measures that might risk the Pyongyang regime's survival.

The *Cheonan* sinking and Yeonpyeong Island shelling (see "North Korean Behavior During Obama Administration" section below) drew the United States even closer to Seoul and, since then, U.S. officials have stated explicitly that they will wait for South Korea's cue to resume negotiations. In 2011, North-South relations took very modest steps forward through some bilateral meetings, but never gained serious momentum. American and South Korean policies appear in complete alignment, with both governments insisting that North Korea demonstrate a serious commitment to implementing the denuclearization aspects of the 2005 Six-Party Talks agreement. U.S.-South Korean cooperation has been underscored by a series of military exercises in the waters surrounding the peninsula, as well as symbolic gestures such as the joint visit of Secretary of State Hillary Clinton and Secretary of Defense Robert Gates to the Demilitarized Zone (DMZ) in June 2010. During the visit, a new set of unilateral U.S. sanctions targeting North Korea was announced.[2]

The Administration has formulated its approach to North Korea against the backdrop of its global nonproliferation agenda. After pledging to work toward a world free of nuclear weapons in an April 2009 speech in Prague, President Obama has taken steps to further that goal, including signing a new nuclear arms reduction treaty with Russia, convening a global leaders' summit to secure stockpiles of nuclear materials, and releasing a new Nuclear Posture Review that outlines new U.S. guidelines on the use of nuclear weapons. The document narrows the circumstances under which nuclear weapons would be used, pledging not to attack nor threaten an attack with nuclear weapons on non-nuclear weapon states that are in compliance with the Nuclear Non-Proliferation Treaty (NPT). When announcing the strategy, officials singled out North Korea and Iran as outliers that are not subject to the security guarantees. The announcement that South Korea plans to host the second Nuclear Security Summit in 2012 further drew attention to Pyongyang's nuclear status.

While the denuclearization talks drag on, the concern about proliferation has intensified. Because of North Korea's dire economic situation, there is a strong fear that it will sell its nuclear technology to another rogue regime or a non-state actor. Evidence of some cooperation with Syria, Iran, and potentially Burma has alarmed national security experts. The Israeli bombing of a nuclear facility in Syria in 2007 raised concern about North Korean collaboration on a nuclear reactor with the Syrians. Reports surface periodically that established commercial relationships in conventional arms sales between Pyongyang and several Middle Eastern countries may have

---

(...continued)

Council Resolution 1874, coordinated by Mary Beth Nikitin and Mark E. Manyin.

[2] For more information, see CRS Report R41438, *North Korea: Legislative Basis for U.S. Economic Sanctions*, by Dianne E. Rennack.

expanded into the nuclear realm as well.[3] The Obama Administration is faced with the question of whether it should pursue limited measures to prevent proliferation in the absence of a "grand bargain" approach to disarm the North.

Food Aid Debate Within U.S. Government

Beginning in early 2011, North Korea issued an appeal for international food aid. A subsequent World Food Program (WFP) assessment reported in March that a quarter of the North Korean population nation is facing severe food shortages due to an unusually cold winter, fertilizer shortages, and rising international food prices. A U.S. delegation, led by Special Envoy for Human Rights in North Korea Robert King, visited the nation in May 2011 to carry out its own assessment. The United States maintains that its food aid policy follows three criteria: demonstrated need, severity of need compared to other countries, and satisfactory monitoring systems to ensure food is reaching the most vulnerable. Obama Administration officials were reportedly divided on whether to authorize new humanitarian assistance for North Korea before a reported agreement to provide aid to North Korea just prior to Kim Jong-il's death. Among critics, strong concerns about diversion of such aid to the elite exist, although assistance provided in 2008-2009 had operated under an improved system of monitoring and access negotiated by the Bush Administration. Another complicating factor involves taking a different stance than South Korea, which explicitly links food aid with diplomatic concerns. Several Members of Congress have spoken out against the provision of any assistance to Pyongyang because of concerns about supporting the regime.

North Korean Behavior During Obama Administration

Since Obama took office, North Korea has emphasized two main demands: that it be recognized as a nuclear weapons state and that a peace treaty with the United States must be a prerequisite to denuclearization. The former demand presents a diplomatic and semantic dilemma: despite repeatedly acknowledging that North Korea has produced nuclear weapons, U.S. officials have insisted that this situation is "unacceptable." According to statements from Pyongyang, the latter demand is an issue of building trust between the United States and North Korea. After years of observing North Korea's negotiating behavior, many analysts believe that such demands are simply tactical moves by Pyongyang and that North Korea has no intention of giving up its nuclear weapons in exchange for aid and recognition. In April 2010, North Korea reiterated its demand to be recognized as an official nuclear weapons state and said it would increase and modernize its nuclear deterrent.

Pattern of Conciliation and Provocations

North Korea's behavior has been erratic since the Obama Administration took office. After its initial string of provocations in 2009, most prominently its May 2009 nuclear test, North Korea appeared to adjust its approach and launched what some dubbed a "charm offensive" strategy. In August 2009, Kim Jong-il received former U.S. President Bill Clinton, after which North Korea released two American journalists who had been held for five months after allegedly crossing the

---

[3] For more information, see CRS Report RL33590, *North Korea's Nuclear Weapons Development and Diplomacy*, by Larry A. Niksch.

border into North Korea. The same month, Kim met with Hyundai Chairperson Hyun Jung-eun. The following month, meetings with Chinese officials yielded encouraging statements about Pyongyang's willingness to rejoin multilateral talks. A North Korean delegation traveled to Seoul for the funeral of former South Korean President Kim Dae-jung and met with President Lee Myung-bak. In early 2010, Pyongyang called for an end to hostilities with the United States and South Korea.

Some observers saw this approach as a product of deteriorating conditions within North Korea. The impact of international sanctions, anxiety surrounding an anticipated leadership succession, and reports of rare social unrest in reaction to a botched attempt at currency reform appeared to be driving Pyongyang's conciliatory gestures. (See "North Korea's Internal Situation" section below.) Many analysts anticipated that North Korea would return to the Six-Party Talks.

String of Provocations in 2010

Expectations of a return to negotiations were altered by the dramatic sinking of the South Korean navy corvette *Cheonan* on March 26, taking the lives of 46 sailors on board. A multinational investigation team led by South Korea determined that the ship was sunk by a torpedo from a North Korean submarine. The Obama Administration expressed staunch support for Seoul and embarked on a series of military exercises to demonstrate its commitment. The attack may have been an effort to shore up support for the succession of Kim Jong-un. According to some analysts, the provocation may have been designed to bolster Kim Jong-il's credibility as a strong leader confronting the South, and therefore his authority to select his son as his replacement.[4]

After the *Cheonan* incident, Pyongyang initiated further provocations. In November, North Korea invited a group of U.S. nuclear experts to the Yongbyon nuclear complex to reveal early construction of an experimental light-water reactor and a small gas centrifuge uranium enrichment facility. The revelations of possible progress toward another path to a nuclear weapon prompted speculation that North Korea was attempting to strengthen its bargaining position if the talks resumed, or perhaps trying to advertise its goods to potential customers. Further, the sophistication of the uranium enrichment plant took many observers by surprise and renewed concerns about Pyongyang's capabilities and deftness in avoiding sanctions to develop its nuclear programs.

On November 23, shortly after announcing its new nuclear facilities, North Korea fired over 170 artillery rounds toward Yeonpyeong Island in the Yellow Sea, killing two ROK Marines and two civilians, injuring many more and damaging multiple structures. The attack, which the North said was a response to South Korean military exercises, was the first since the Korean War to strike South Korean territory directly and inflict civilian casualties. Again, the U.S. military joined the ROK for military exercises, this time deploying the USS *George Washington* aircraft carrier to the Yellow Sea. Despite Pyongyang's threats of retaliation, South Korea staged its previously scheduled live fire exercises near Yeonpyeong Island, prompting an emergency meeting of the United Nations Security Council amid fear of the outbreak of war. Perhaps due to Chinese pressure, the North refrained from responding.

---

[4] "U.S. Implicates North Korean Leader in Attack," *New York Times.* May 22, 2010.

Reaching Out Again in 2011

In early 2011, Pyongyang appeared to be re-launching a diplomatic offensive and ceased to initiate more provocations, presumably to secure new economic assistance and food aid. Pyongyang welcomed foreign delegations, including the Elders group led by former U.S. President Jimmy Carter and a U.S. team led by Special Envoy for Human Rights in North Korea Ambassador Robert King. Leader Kim Jong-il visited China four times in his last 20 months with his itineraries heavy on stops that showcase Chinese economic development. China had urged Kim to embrace economic reform for years; some analysts saw the repeated trips as an indication that he sought further aid and support from Beijing, as well as perhaps to secure support for his successor. Although rhetoric toward the South remained harsh, Pyongyang engaged in some initial North-South dialogue sessions.

Six-Party Talks

Background: History of Negotiations

North Korea's nuclear weapons programs have concerned the United States for nearly three decades. In the 1980s, U.S. intelligence detected new construction of a nuclear reactor at Yongbyon. In the early 1990s, after agreeing to and then obstructing IAEA inspections, North Korea announced its intention to withdraw from the Nuclear Non-Proliferation Treaty (NPT).[5] According to statements by former Clinton Administration officials, a pre-emptive military strike on the North's nuclear facilities was seriously considered as the crisis developed.[6] Discussion of sanctions at the United Nations Security Council and a diplomatic mission from former President Jimmy Carter diffused the tension and eventually led to the 1994 Agreed Framework, an agreement between the United States and North Korea that essentially would have provided two light water reactors (LWRs) and heavy fuel oil to North Korea in exchange for a freeze of its plutonium program. The document also outlined a path toward normalization of diplomatic relations.

Beset by problems from the start, the agreement faced multiple delays in funding from the U.S. side and a lack of compliance by the North Koreans. Still, the fundamentals of the agreement were implemented: North Korea froze its plutonium program, heavy fuel oil was delivered to the North Koreans, and LWR construction commenced. In 2002, U.S. officials confronted North Korea about a suspected uranium enrichment program, dealing a further blow to the agreement. After minimal progress in construction of the LWRs, the project was suspended in 2003. After North Korea expelled inspectors from the Yongbyon site and announced its withdrawal from the NPT, the project was officially terminated in January 2006.

Under the George W. Bush Administration, the negotiations to resolve the North Korean nuclear issue expanded to include China, South Korea, Japan, and Russia. With China playing host, six rounds of the "Six-Party Talks" from 2003-2007 yielded occasional incremental progress, but

---

[5] Walter Pincus, "Nuclear Conflict Has Deep Roots: 50 Years of Threats and Broken Pacts Culminate in Apparent Nuclear Test," *Washington Post*. October 15, 2006.

[6] "Washington was on Brink of War with North Korea 5 Years Ago," *CNN.com*. October 4, 1999 and North Korea Nuclear Crisis, February 1993 - June 1994," *GlobalSecurity.org*.

ultimately failed to resolve the fundamental issue of North Korean nuclear arms. The most promising breakthrough occurred in 2005, with the issuance of a Joint Statement in which North Korea agreed to abandon its nuclear weapons programs in exchange for aid, a U.S. security guarantee, and normalization of relations with the United States. Some observers described the agreement as "Agreed Framework Plus." Despite the promise of the statement, the process eventually broke down due to complications over the release of North Korean assets from a bank in Macau and then degenerated further with North Korea's test of a nuclear device in October 2006.[7]

In February 2007, Six-Party Talks negotiators announced an agreement that would provide economic and diplomatic benefits to North Korea in exchange for a freeze and disablement of Pyongyang's nuclear facilities. This was followed by an October 2007 agreement that more specifically laid out the implementation plans, including the disablement of the Yongbyon facility, a North Korean declaration of its nuclear programs, and a U.S. promise to lift economic sanctions on North Korea and remove North Korea from the U.S. list of state sponsors of terrorism. Under the leadership of Assistant Secretary of State for East Asia and Pacific Affairs Christopher Hill, the Bush Administration pushed ahead for a deal, including removing North Korea from the terrorism list in October 2008.[8] Disagreements over the verification protocol between Washington and Pyongyang stalled the process until the U.S. presidential election in November 2008.

Multilateral negotiations on North Korea's nuclear program have not been held since December 2008. Pyongyang's refusal to take responsibility for the *Cheonan* sinking has left the international nuclear negotiations frozen. Seoul has insisted that North Korea must apologize for the incident, as well as show "sincerity" in implementing major denuclearization commitments made in the 2005 landmark accord among the six nations. China has worked aggressively behind the scenes to restart the negotiations, but the United States has remained steadfast that an improvement in North-South relations is a pre-requisite for forward movement on the talks. Hopes for a resumption of the negotiations have risen periodically, including when former U.S. President Jimmy Carter visited North Korea in April 2011 along with three other former leaders from the group "The Elders." North Korea claims to be willing to return to the talks "without preconditions," but U.S. and other officials point to Pyongyang's failure to implement previous agreements.

China's Role

As host of the Six-Party Talks and as North Korea's chief benefactor, China plays a crucial role in the negotiations. Beijing's decision to host the talks marked China's most significant foray onto the international diplomatic stage and was counted as a significant achievement by the Bush Administration. Formation of the six-nation format, initiated by the Bush Administration in 2002 and continued under the Obama Administration, confirms the critical importance of China's role in U.S. policy toward North Korea. The United States depends on Beijing's leverage to relay messages to the North Koreans, push Pyongyang for concessions and attendance at the negotiations, and, on some occasions, punish the North for its actions. In addition, China's

---

[7] For more details on problems with implementation and verification, see CRS Report RL33590, *North Korea's Nuclear Weapons Development and Diplomacy*, by Larry A. Niksch.

[8] For more information on the terrorism list removal, see CRS Report RL30613, *North Korea: Back on the Terrorism List?* by Mark E. Manyin.

permanent seat on the United Nations Security Council ensures its influence on any U.N. action directed at North Korea.

In addition to being North Korea's largest trading partner by far, China also provides considerable concessional assistance. The large amount of food and energy aid that China supplies is an essential lifeline for the regime in Pyongyang, particularly since the cessation of most aid from South Korea under the Lee Administration. It is clear that Beijing cannot control Pyongyang's behavior—particularly in the cases of provocative nuclear tests and missile launches—but even temporary cessation of economic and energy aid is significant for North Korea. In September 2006, Chinese trade statistics reflected a temporary cut-off in oil exports to North Korea, in a period which followed several provocative missile tests by Pyongyang. Although Beijing did not label the reduction as a punishment, some analysts saw the move as a reflection of China's displeasure with the North's actions.[9] In instances when the international community wishes to condemn Pyongyang's behavior, such as the sanctions imposed in U.N. Security Council Resolution 1874, Beijing's willingness to punish the regime largely determines how acutely North Korea is affected.

China's overriding priority of preventing North Korea's collapse remains firm.[10] Beijing fears the destabilizing effects of a humanitarian crisis, significant refugee flows over its borders, and the uncertainty of how other nations, particularly the United States, would assert themselves on the peninsula in the event of a power vacuum. While focusing on its own economic development, China favors the maintenance of regional stability over all other concerns. In an effort to shore up the new regime in Pyongyang, Beijing has rushed to support Kim Jong-un and, in doing so, legitimize the new leader. To try to stabilize North Korea's economy, China is expanding economic ties and supporting joint industrial projects between China's northeastern provinces and North Korea's northern border region. Many Chinese leaders also see strategic value in having North Korea as a "buffer" between it and the democratic, U.S.-allied South Korea.

North Korea's Internal Situation

The remarkable durability of the North Korean regime despite its intense isolation and economic dysfunction may be undergoing its biggest test. Kim Jong-il's death, the questions surrounding how Kim Jong-un will lead the country, and continued food shortages have heightened uncertainty about the regime's future. In addition, the impact of international sanctions and the virtual cessation of aid from Seoul under the Lee Administration leaves the government with limited options for providing for the elite and holding on to power.

The North Korean regime remains extraordinarily opaque, but a trickle of news works its way out through North Korean exiles and other channels. These forms of grass-roots information gathering have democratized the business of intelligence on North Korea. Previously, South Korean intelligence services had generally provided the bulk of information known about the North. Surveys of North Korean defectors reveal that some within North Korea are growing increasingly wary of government propaganda and turning to outside sources of news.[11]

---

[9] "China Cut Off Exports of Oil to North Korea," *New York Times*. October 30, 2006.

[10] For more information, please see CRS Report R41043, *China-North Korea Relations*, by Dick K. Nanto and Mark E. Manyin.

[11] Marcus Noland, "Pyongyang Tipping Point," *Wall Street Journal* op-ed. April 12, 2010.

Succession Process

Anticipation surrounding the now unfolding succession process has been the subject of furious speculation since Kim Jong-il suffered a stroke in August 2008. Formal evidence of the selection of Kim Jong-un emerged in 2010, when the younger Kim was appointed as a four-star general as well as a vice-chairman of the Central Military Commission, a powerful organ of the Korean Workers Party (KPA). He also became a member of the Central Committee of the KPA. He later appeared by his father's side during military exercises and, following the death of a prominent military figure, was named to the state funeral committee, again indicating his elevated status. In September 2010, a rare session of the Supreme People's Assembly confirmed that the regime was preparing to transfer leadership. Many analysts believed that the regime aimed for a formal appointment in 2012 because it marks North Korean founder Kim Il-sung's 100th birthday, and was the year designated by Kim Jong-il for North Korea to become "militarily strong and economically prosperous."

The haste surrounding the succession is in marked contrast to the transfer of power to Kim Jong-il after his father Kim Il-sung's sudden death in 1994: Kim Jong-il had been publicly groomed as the inheritor of his father's position for several years. The risks of pulling off a dynastic succession are high, although the process since Kim Jong-il's death appears to be remarkably smooth, particularly in light of the fact that he passed suddenly. Though he looked frail and required support to walk at his last handful of public appearances, many observers noted that his condition did not seem as dire as some had suggested.

Although Kim Jong-un was clearly being established as the next leader when his father passed, he is still relatively unfamiliar to the public, making many analysts question whether the North Korean people ultimately will embrace his leadership. Perhaps more importantly, Kim Jong-un's legitimacy among the established power constituencies may be tenuous. Other senior figures were elevated when he first received high-profile promotions, leading to speculation that the young Kim is buffeted by a group of close advisors. Most prominently, Kim Jong-il's brother-in-law, Jang Song-taek, earlier was appointed as vice-chairman of the National Defense Commission, making him second in command under Kim Jong-il. Analysts speculate that Jang could serve as a regent with Kim Jong-un as the bloodline figurehead. Kim Kyong-hui, Jang's wife and Kim Jong-il's sister, also received promotions in the military and political elite. Because of Kim's youth and inexperience, it appears that a group of senior advisors may serve as a collective leadership.

Kim Jong-un's and others' appointments to high-level party positions have led some analysts to posit that the Korean Workers' Party may be gaining in stature over the military establishment. The emphasis on the Central Military Commission, the tool through which the Party controls the military, may indicate that the regime is moving away from the concentrated power in the National Defense Commission exploited by Kim Jong-il and instead returning to a Party-centric order, as was the case under Kim Il-sung. The *Songun*, or "Military First," policy is likely to remain in place, but Kim Jong-un may seek to establish his authority over the military by developing authority within the Party.[12] The September conclave highlighted the restoration of several formal Party organs as the mechanism through which a new generation would rise.[13]

---

[12] "Amid Leadership Reshuffle, Role of Central Military Commission Strengthens in N. Korea," *Hankyoreh*, September 30, 2010.

[13] Ruediger Frank, "Hu Jintao, Deng Xiapoing or Another Mao Zedong? Power Restructuring in North Korea," *38 North*. November 2010. (http://38north.org/2010/10/1451/)

The implications for the United States of how succession planning proceeds are significant. Many analysts point to the danger of a power vacuum in a state with a nuclear arsenal, with competing elements possibly locked in a struggle against one another. However destructive Kim Jong-il was, his leadership has provided a degree of stability. The scenarios of collective leadership, dynastic succession, or foreign intervention all present tremendous risks that could disrupt existing channels of negotiation with North Korea. Though some hold out hope that the young, European-educated Kim could emerge as a reformer, most analysts conclude that the North's outdated ideology and closed political system will not allow for divergence on the part of the new leader.[14]

Solidifying Ties with China

As North Korea prepared for the end of the Kim Jong-il era, the regime appeared to draw closer to China. This process took form in both internal party-to-party interactions as well as on the international scene. In early May 2010, as South Korean President Lee Myung-bak's administration weighed how to respond to the *Cheonan* sinking without risking an escalation into general war, Kim Jong-il visited China for the first time in four years, a move that infuriated Seoul. Beijing resisted U.S. and others' appeals to condemn the attack, including fighting for language in a United Nations Security Council statement that avoided directly blaming North Korea. Kim returned to China in August 2010, May 2011, and August 2011. Observers speculated that Kim was seeking China's support for his son's succession, as well as perhaps more food aid.

The possible increase in the Korean Workers' Party power in Pyongyang's decision-making process has implications for China's influence. Analysts have noted deepening links between the Korean Worker's Party and the Communist Party in China. Some analysts have identified Beijing's pursuit of economic cooperation with North Korea—including the provision of capital and development of natural resources within North Korea—as channeled through the Communist Party of China (CPC) International Liaison Department, that is, through party-to-party engagement.[15] If indeed the KWP's power becomes paramount in Pyongyang, Beijing could stand to increase its clout.

Both sides have some reservations about becoming too interlinked: Beijing faces condemnation from the international community, and deterioration of relations with an important trade partner in South Korea, for defending North Korea, and Pyongyang seeks to avoid complete dependence on China to preserve some degree of autonomy. However, both capitals appear to have calculated that their strategic interests—or, in the case of Pyongyang, survival—depend on the other.

Other U.S. Concerns with North Korea

North Korea's Human Rights Record

Although the nuclear issue has dominated relations with Pyongyang, U.S. officials periodically voice concerns about North Korea's very poor human rights record. The plight of most North

---

[14] Victor Cha, "Without a Loosened Grip, Reform will Elude North Korea," *CSIS Korea Platform*. October 15, 2010.

[15] John Park, "On the Issues: North Korea's Leadership Succession: The China Factor." *United States Institute of Peace* (http://www.usip.org). September 28, 2010.

Koreans is dire. The State Department's annual human rights reports and reports from private organizations have portrayed a little-changing pattern of extreme human rights abuses by the North Korea regime over many years.[16] The reports stress a total denial of political, civil, and religious liberties and say that no dissent or criticism of leadership is allowed. Freedoms of speech, the press, and assembly do not exist. There is no independent judiciary, and citizens do not have the right to choose their own government. Reports also document the extensive ideological indoctrination of North Korean citizens.

Severe physical abuse is meted out to citizens who violate laws and restrictions. Multiple reports have described a system of prison camps that house 150,000 to 200,000 inmates, including many political prisoners.[17] Reports from survivors and escapees from the camps indicate that conditions in the camps for political prisoners are extremely harsh and that many political prisoners do not survive. Reports cite executions and torture of prisoners as a frequent practice.

A 2011 study of DPRK defectors indicates that in recent years many North Koreans have been arrested for what would earlier have been deemed ordinary economic activities. North Korea criminalizes market activities, seeing them as a set of challenges to the state. Its penal system targets low-level or misdemeanor crimes, such as unsanctioned trading or violations of travel permits. Violators face detention in local-level "collection centers" and "labor training centers." Defectors have reported starvation, suffered beatings and torture, and witnessed executions in these centers.[18]

In addition to the extreme curtailment of rights, many North Koreans face significant food shortages. In a recent survey, the World Food Program identified urgent hunger needs for 3.5 million citizens in North Korea, out of a total population of 24 million. UNICEF has reported that each year some 40,000 North Korean children under five became "acutely malnourished," with 25,000 needing hospital treatment. About one-third of the population reportedly suffers from stunting.[19]

North Korean Refugees

For over a decade, food shortages, persecution, and human rights abuses have prompted perhaps hundreds of thousands of North Koreans to go to neighboring China, where they are forced to evade Chinese security forces and often become victims of further abuse, neglect, and lack of protection. There is little reliable information on the size and composition of the North Korean population located in China. Estimates range up to 300,000 or more. The United Nations High Commissioner for Refugees (UNHCR) has not been given access to conduct a systematic survey. Reports indicate that many women and children are the victims of human trafficking, particularly

---

[16] See U.S. Department of State, 2010 Country Report on Human Rights Practices: Democratic People's Republic of Korea, April 2011, available at http://www.state.gov/g/drl/rls/hrrpt/2010/eap/154388.htm, and Amnesty International Annual Report 2011 - North Korea, available at http://www.unhcr.org/refworld/country,COI,,,PRK,4562d8cf2,4dce154c3c,0.html.

[17] Radio Free Asia, North Korea: "Political Prison Camps Expand," May 4, 2011, available at http://www.unhcr.org/refworld/docid/4dd288f128 html.

[18] Stephan Haggard and Marcus Noland, *Witness to Transformation, Refugee Insights into North Korea* (Peterson Institute for International Economics, 2011), p. 51.

[19] Amnesty International, Amnesty International Annual Report 2011 - North Korea, May 13, 2011, available at http://www.unhcr.org/refworld/docid/4dce154c3c html.

women lured to China seeking a better life but forced into marriage or prostitution.[20] Some of the refugees who escape to China make their way to Southeast Asia or Mongolia, where they may seek passage to a third country, usually South Korea. If repatriated, they risk harsh punishment or execution.

The North Korean Human Rights Act

In 2004, the 108th Congress passed, and President George W. Bush signed, the North Korean Human Rights Act (H.R. 4011; P.L. 108-333). Among its chief goals are the promotion and protection of human rights in North Korea and the creation of a "durable humanitarian" option for its refugees. The North Korean Human Rights Act (NKHRA) authorized new funds to support human rights efforts and improve the flow of information, and required the President to appoint a Special Envoy on human rights in North Korea. Under the NKHRA, North Koreans may apply for asylum in the United States, and the State Department is required to facilitate the submission of their applications. The bill required that all non-humanitarian assistance must be linked to improvements in human rights, but provided a waiver if the President deems the aid to be in the interest of national security.

In 2008, Congress reauthorized NKHRA under P.L. 110-346 at the original levels of $2 million annually to support human rights and democracy programs, $2 million annually to promote freedom of information programs for North Koreans, and $20 million annually to assist North Korean refugees. Appropriations for the reauthorization were extended to 2012. The legislation also requires additional reporting on U.S. efforts to resettle North Korean refugees in the United States.

Implementation

Relatively few North Korean refugees have resettled in the United States. According to the State Department, as of May 2011, 120 North Korean refugees now reside in the United States.[21] The Government Accountability Office (GAO) reports that in spite of the U.S. government's efforts to expand resettlements, rates did not improve from 2006-2008.[22] Several U.S. agencies were involved in working with other countries to resettle such refuges, but North Korean applicants face hurdles. Some host countries delay the granting of exit permissions or limit contacts with U.S. officials. Other host governments are reluctant to antagonize Pyongyang by admitting North Korean refugees and prefer to avoid making their countries known as a reliable transit points. Another challenge is educating the North Korean refugee population about the potential to resettle in the United States, many of whom may not be aware of the program.

Under the NKHRA, Congress authorized $2 million annually to promote freedom of information programs for North Koreans. It called on the Broadcasting Board of Governors (BBG) to "facilitate the unhindered dissemination of information in North Korea" by increasing Korean-language broadcasts by Radio Free Asia (RFA) and Voice of America (VOA).[23] A modest amount

---

[20] United States Department of State, Trafficking in Persons Report 2010 - Korea, Democratic People's Republic of, June 14, 2010, available at http://www.unhcr.org/refworld/docid/4c1883e6c html.

[21] CRS email correspondence with U.S. Department of State, May 26, 2011.

[22] U.S. Government Accountability Office, *Humanitarian Assistance: Status of North Korean Refugee Resettlement and Asylum in the United States*, GAO-10-691, June 24, 2010, available at http://www.gao.gov.

[23] Broadcast content includes news briefs, particularly news about the Korean Peninsula; interviews with North Korean (continued...)

has been appropriated to support independent radio broadcasters. The BBG currently broadcasts to North Korea ten hours per day. In FY2010, the BBG spent $8.49 million to cover the cost of transmission as well as of a news center for VOA Seoul and the RFA Seoul Bureau. For FY2011, it requested $8.46 million which includes funding for the VOA and RFA Bureaus.[24] Although official North Korean radios are altered by the government to prevent outside broadcasts, defectors report that many citizens have illegal radios that receive the programs. There have also been efforts in the past by the U.S. and South Korean governments to smuggle in radios in order to allow information to penetrate the closed country.

In 2009, Robert R. King, a long-time aide to the late Representative Tom Lantos, became the Obama Administration's Special Envoy on North Korean Human Rights Issues. Before joining the Administration, he was involved in the planning of Representative Lantos' human rights agenda, visited North Korea and played a role in the passage of the NKHRA. King is currently leading a mission to North Korea to assess the need for humanitarian food aid, as well as raise broader human rights issues with North Korean officials. His trip is the first by a Special Envoy on North Korea Human Rights to the country since the creation of the post under the 2004 law. According to the State Department, King's office is closely integrated with the Office of the Special Envoy on North Korea, Stephen W. Bosworth. As a result, he consults regularly with his counterparts in the Department and he works on a full-time basis. The office of the former Special Envoy, Jay Lefkowitz, fell under the Bureau of Democracy, Human Rights, and Labor. Lefkowitz worked on a part-time basis, which drew criticism from some Members of Congress.

North Korea's Illicit Activities

Strong indications exist that the North Korean regime has been involved in the production and trafficking of illicit drugs, as well as of counterfeit currency, cigarettes, and pharmaceuticals. DPRK crime-for-profit activities have reportedly brought in important foreign currency resources and come under the direction of a special office under the direction of the ruling Korean Worker's Party.[25] Although U.S. policy during the first term of the Bush Administration highlighted these activities, they have generally been relegated since to a lower level of priority compared to the nuclear issue.

In September 2005, the U.S. Treasury Department identified Banco Delta Asia, located in Macau, as a bank that distributed North Korean counterfeit currency and allowed for money laundering for North Korean criminal enterprises. It ordered the freezing of $24 million in North Korean accounts with the bank. This action prompted many other banks to freeze North Korean accounts and derailed potential progress on the September 2005 Six-Party Talks agreement. After lengthy

---

(...continued)

defectors; and international commentary on events occurring in North Korea. The BBG cites a Peterson Institute for International Economics survey in which North Korean defectors interviewed in China and South Korea indicated that they had listened to foreign media including RFA. RFA broadcasts five hours a day. VOA broadcasts five hours a day with three of those hours in prime-time from a medium-wave transmitter in South Korea aimed at North Korea. VOA also broadcasts from stations in Thailand; the Philippines; and from leased stations in Russia and eastern Mongolia. In January 2009, the BBG began broadcasting to North Korea from a leased medium-wave facility in South Korea. The BBG added leased transmission capability to bolster medium-wave service into North Korea in January 2010. RFA broadcasts from stations in Tinian (Northern Marianas) and Saipan, and leased stations in Russia and Mongolia.

[24] Data on funding supplied by the Broadcasting Board of Governors, November 8, 2010.

[25] For more information, see CRS Report RL33885, *North Korean Crime-for-Profit Activities*, by Liana Sun Wyler and Dick K. Nanto.

negotiations and complicated arrangements, in June 2007 the Bush Administration agreed to allow the release of the $24 million from Banco Delta Asia accounts and ceased its campaign to pressure foreign governments and banks to avoid doing business with North Korea. Since the second nuclear test and the passage of U.N. Security Resolution 1874, there have been renewed efforts to pressure Pyongyang through the restriction of illicit activities, particularly arms sales.

North Korea's Missile Program

North Korea has a well-developed missile program, as evidenced by its repeated tests over the past several years.[26] The missiles have not been a high priority for U.S. North Korea policy since the late Clinton Administration and have not been on the agenda in the Six-Party Talks. In 1999, North Korea agreed to a moratorium on long-range missile tests in exchange for the Clinton Administration's pledge to lift certain economic sanctions. The deal was later abandoned during the Bush Administration. In 2006, U.N. Security Council Resolution 1718 barred North Korea from conducting missile-related activities. North Korea flouted this resolution with its April 2009 test of the long-range Taepodong II.

According to South Korean defense officials, Pyongyang's arsenal includes intermediate-range missiles that have a range of about 1,860 miles, which includes all of Japan and the U.S. military bases located there.[27] Some military analysts believe that North Korea is close to deploying ballistic missiles that could eventually threaten the west coast of the continental United States. Pyongyang has sold missile parts and technology to several states, including Egypt, Iran, Libya, Pakistan, Syria, United Arab Emirates, and Yemen.[28] Of key concern to the United States is the North Koreans' ability to successfully miniaturize nuclear warheads and mount them on ballistic missiles. Military experts have cited progress in North Korea's missile development as evidenced by its tests. They note that the April 2009 test of the Taepodong II, which Pyongyang claimed was a satellite launch, failed but still indicated advancements in long-range missile technology.[29]

During a visit to China in January 2011, U.S. Secretary of Defense Robert Gates called for missile and nuclear testing moratoria by North Korea and said that while the North Korean missile threat to the United States will be "very limited" in five years, it is still cause for concern. Press reports in mid-February 2011 showed a completed launch pad and launch tower at a second missile launch facility in North Korea's northwest, close to the border with China, near Tongchang-dong. The DPRK has been constructing the site, a more sophisticated set-up than the current launch facility at Musudan-ri, for the past decade, and analysts say it could be used to test inter-continental ballistic missiles.

---

[26] For more information, see CRS Report RS21473, *North Korean Ballistic Missile Threat to the United States*, by Steven A. Hildreth.

[27] "North Korea Has 1,000 Missiles, South Says," *Reuters*, March 16, 2010.

[28] *Jane's Sentinel Security Assessment - China And Northeast Asia*, January 22, 2010.

[29] David Wright and Theordore A. Postol, "A Post-launch Examination of the Unha-2," *Bulletin of the Atomic Scientists*. June 29, 2009.

U.S. Engagement Activities with North Korea

U.S. Assistance to North Korea[30]

Since 1995, the United States has provided North Korea with over $1.2 billion in assistance, of which about 60% has paid for food aid and about 40% for energy assistance. Except for a small ongoing medical assistance program, the United States has not provided any aid to North Korea since early 2009; the United States provided all of its share of pledged heavy fuel oil by December 2008. Energy assistance was tied to progress in the Six-Party Talks, which broke down in 2009. U.S. food aid, which officially is not linked to diplomatic developments, ended in early 2009 due to disagreements with Pyongyang over monitoring and access. (The North Korean government restricts the ability of donors to operate in the country.) In 2011, North Korea issued appeals to the international community for additional food aid (see "" section above).

From 2007 to April 2009, the United States also provided technical assistance to North Korea to help in the nuclear disablement process. In 2008, Congress took legislative steps to legally enable the President to give expanded assistance for this purpose. However, following North Korea's actions in the spring of 2009 when it test-fired a missile, tested a nuclear device, halted denuclearization activities, and expelled nuclear inspectors, Congress explicitly rejected the Obama Administration's requests for funds to supplement existing resources in the event of a breakthrough in the Six-Party Talks. Prior to the spring of 2010, the Obama Administration and the Lee Myung-bak government in South Korea had said that they would be willing to provide large-scale aid if North Korea took steps to irreversibly dismantle its nuclear program.

POW-MIA Recovery Operations in North Korea

In 1994, North Korea invited the U.S. government to conduct joint investigations to recover the remains of thousands of U.S. servicemen unaccounted for during the Korean War. The United Nations Military Command (U.N. Command) and the Korean People's Army conducted 33 joint investigations from 1996-2005 for these prisoners of war-missing in action (POW-MIAs). In operations known as "joint field activities" (JFAs), U.S. specialists recovered 229 sets of remains and successfully identified 78 of those. On May 25, 2005, the Department of Defense announced that it would suspend all JFAs, citing the "uncertain environment created by North Korea's unwillingness to participate in the six-party talks" concerning North Korea's nuclear program, its recent declarations regarding its intentions to develop nuclear weapons, and its withdrawal from the nuclear nonproliferation treaty, and the payments of millions of dollars in cash to the Korean People's Army (KPA) for its help in recovering the remains.[31]

The United States has not undertaken any JFAs with the KPA since May 2005. On January 27, 2010, the KPA proposed that the United States and North Korea resume talks on the joint recovery program. On April 5, the KPA issued a public statement criticizing the Department of Defense for failing to accept its proposal. It said the DPRK would not assume responsibility for the loss of remains because of delays in the Six-Party Talks, specifically: "If thousands of U.S. remains buried in our country are washed off and lost due to the U.S. side's disregard, the U.S.

[30] For more, see CRS Report R40095, *Foreign Assistance to North Korea*, by Mark E. Manyin and Mary Beth Nikitin.
[31]"U.S. Halts Search for Its War Dead in North Korea," *New York Times.* May 26, 2005.

side should be wholly responsible for the consequences as it has developed the humanitarian issue into a political problem."[32] The Department of Defense has said that the recovery of the remains of missing U.S. soldiers is an enduring priority goal of the United States and that it is committed to achieving the fullest possible accounting for POW-MIAs from the Korean War.

Potential for Establishing a Liaison Office in North Korea

One prospective step for engagement would be the establishment of a liaison office in Pyongyang. This issue has waxed and waned over the past 16 years. The Clinton Administration, as part of the 1994 U.S.-North Korea Agreed Framework, outlined the possibility of full normalization of political and economic relations. Under the Agreed Framework, the United States and North Korea would open a liaison office in each other's capital "following resolution of consular and other technical issues through expert level discussions."[33] Eventually, the relationship would have been upgraded to "bilateral relations [at] the Ambassadorial level." Under the Bush Administration, Ambassador Christopher Hill reportedly discussed an exchange of liaison offices. This did not lead to an offer of full diplomatic relations pursuant to negotiations in the Six-Party Talks. In December 2009, following Ambassador Stephen Bosworth's first visit as Special Envoy to Pyongyang, press speculation ran high that the United States would offer relations at the level of liaison offices. The Obama Administration quickly dispelled these expectations, flatly rejecting claims that Bosworth had carried a message offering liaison offices.[34]

Non-Governmental Organizations' Activities

Since the reported famines in North Korea of the mid-1990s, the largest proportion of aid has come from government contributions to emergency relief programs administered by international relief organizations. Some non-governmental organizations (NGOs) are playing smaller roles in capacity building and people-to-people exchanges, in areas such as health, informal diplomacy, information science, and education.

The aims of such NGOs are as diverse as the institutions themselves. Some illustrative cases include NGO "joint ventures" between scientific and academic NGOs and those engaged in informal diplomacy. Three consortia highlight this cooperation: the Tuberculosis (TB) diagnostics project, run by Nuclear Threat Initiative (NTI), Stanford Medical School, and Christian Friends of Korea; the Syracuse University-Kim Chaek University of Technology digital library program; and the U.S.-DPRK Scientific Engagement Consortium, composed of the Civilian Research and Development Foundation Global (CRDF Global), the American Association for the Advancement of Science (AAAS), Syracuse University, and the Korea Society. The following is a sample of such efforts.

- In 2008, NTI, Stanford Medical School, and Christian Friends identified multiple drug resistant TB as a serious security threat. By providing North Korean

---

[32] "KPA Holds US Side Responsible for Leaving Remains of GIs," *Korean Central News Agency* (KCNA), April 5, 2010.

[33] 1994 US-DPRK Agreed Framework at http://www.kedo.org/pdfs/AgreedFramework.pdf.

[34] "U.S. has not proposed setting up liaison office in Pyongyang next year: White House." *Yonhap*, December 19, 2009 (Lexis-Nexis).

scientists with the scientific equipment, generators, and other supplies to furnish a national tuberculosis reference laboratory, they hope to enable North Korean researchers and physicians to take on this health threat.[35] Over the course of 2010, the partners completed the TB reference laboratory, and installed a high voltage cable for more regular energy supply.[36] In September 2010, North Korea health representatives signed a grant agreement for a two-year period with the Global Fund to Fight AIDS, Tuberculosis, and Malaria. The $19 million dollar grant will support procurement of laboratory supplies as well as vaccines through July 2012.

- In 2001, Syracuse University and Kim Chaek University (Pyongyang) began a modest program of modifying open-source software for use as library support and identifying the international standards necessary to catalog information for the library at Kim Chaek. Over time this expanded to include twin integrated information technology labs at Kim Chaek and Syracuse and a memorandum to exchange junior faculty. North Korean junior faculty members are expected to attend Syracuse University in spring 2011.[37]

- In 2007, the U.S.-DPRK Scientific Engagement Consortium formed to explore collaborative science activities between the United States and North Korea in subjects such as agriculture and information technology. In December 2009, at the invitation of the North Korean State Academy of Sciences, Consortium members toured facilities and received briefings from researchers in biology, alternative energy, information sciences, hydrology, and health. Potential areas for collaboration include identification of shared research priorities, academic exchanges, joint workshops on English language, mathematics, biomedical research methods, renewable energy and digital science libraries, and joint science publications.

List of Other CRS Reports on North Korea

CRS Report RL34256, *North Korea's Nuclear Weapons: Technical Issues*, by Mary Beth Nikitin

CRS Report R41481, *U.S.-South Korea Relations*, coordinated by Mark E. Manyin

CRS Report R42126, *Kim Jong-il's Death: Implications for North Korea's Stability and U.S. Policy*, by Mark E. Manyin

CRS Report R40095, *Foreign Assistance to North Korea*, by Mark E. Manyin and Mary Beth Nikitin

CRS Report R40684, *North Korea's Second Nuclear Test: Implications of U.N. Security Council Resolution 1874*, coordinated by Mary Beth Nikitin and Mark E. Manyin

---

[35] "New Tuberculosis Lab Hailed as Breakthrough in Health Diplomacy." *Science*. March 12, 2010. p. 1312-1313.

[36] Christian Friends of Newsletter, November 2010.

[37] Hyunjin Seo and Stuart Thorson. "Academic Science Engagement with North Korea." *On Korea*. Washington, DC: Korea Economic Institute of America, 2010. p. 105-121.

CRS Report R41438, *North Korea: Legislative Basis for U.S. Economic Sanctions*, by Dianne E. Rennack

CRS Report RL30613, *North Korea: Back on the Terrorism List?*, by Mark E. Manyin

CRS Report R41160, *North Korea's 2009 Nuclear Test: Containment, Monitoring, Implications*, by Jonathan Medalia

CRS Report RL32493, *North Korea: Economic Leverage and Policy Analysis*, by Dick K. Nanto and Emma Chanlett-Avery

CRS Report RS22973, *Congress and U.S. Policy on North Korean Human Rights and Refugees: Recent Legislation and Implementation*, by Emma Chanlett-Avery

CRS Report RL33324, *North Korean Counterfeiting of U.S. Currency*, by Dick K. Nanto

CRS Report R41043, *China-North Korea Relations*, by Dick K. Nanto and Mark E. Manyin

CRS Report RS21473, *North Korean Ballistic Missile Threat to the United States*, by Steven A. Hildreth

Archived Reports for Background

CRS Report RL33567, *Korea-U.S. Relations: Issues for Congress*, by Larry A. Niksch

CRS Report RL33590, *North Korea's Nuclear Weapons Development and Diplomacy*, by Larry A. Niksch

CRS Report RL31696, *North Korea: Economic Sanctions Prior to Removal from Terrorism Designation*, by Dianne E. Rennack

Author Contact Information

Emma Chanlett-Avery
Specialist in Asian Affairs
echanlettavery@crs.loc.gov, 7-7748

Acknowledgments

Mi Ae Taylor, formerly a Research Associate in Asian Affairs, contributed to the preparation of this report.